This book, titled **"Harmony and Equity: A Comprehensive Exploration of Social Justice in Islam"**, along with its contents encompassing text, illustrations, images, diagrams, and other creative elements, is the exclusive property of BINISH SHAH and is safeguarded by copyright law.

BINISH SHAH asserts full ownership and retains all rights to this book. No part of this publication may be reproduced, distributed, or transmitted in any form or by any means, such as photocopying, recording, or electronic methods, without prior written consent from the copyright holder. Brief quotations in critical reviews and certain noncommercial uses permitted by copyright law are exceptions.

This copyright notice applies to all editions, formats, and translations of the book, whether in print, digital, or any other medium or technology existing now or developed in the future. Unauthorized use or infringement may result in legal action and pursuit of remedies under applicable copyright laws.

While efforts have been made to ensure accuracy and reliability, BINISH SHAH does not guarantee the completeness or suitability of the information. Readers are responsible for evaluating and using the content judiciously.

BINISH SHAH reserves the right to make changes, updates, or corrections to the book without prior notice. Inclusion of third-party materials or references does not imply endorsement or affiliation unless used under fair use principles or with proper permissions and attributions.

For permissions, inquiries, or requests regarding the book's use, please contact BINISH SHAH through official channels listed on their Amazon author page or provided email address.

This comprehensive copyright notice serves to protect BINISH SHAH's intellectual property rights, maintain content control, and inform users about associated restrictions and permissions.

Warm regards,

BINISH SHAH

Harmony and Equity

A Comprehensive Exploration of

SOCIAL JUSTICE IN ISLAM

Table of Content

Preface:

In the name of Allah, the Most Gracious, the Most Merciful.

Praise be to Allah, the Lord of all worlds, and peace and blessings be upon the Prophet Muhammad (peace be upon him) and his family and companions.

The concept of social justice is deeply rooted in the teachings of Islam. From its inception, Islam has emphasized the importance of justice, fairness, and equity in all aspects of life. The Quran and the teachings of the Prophet Muhammad (peace be upon him) are replete with verses and Hadiths that highlight the importance of social justice and the duty of Muslims to uphold it.

"Harmony and Equity: A Comprehensive Exploration of Social Justice in Islam" is a humble attempt to delve into the rich teachings of Islam regarding social justice. This book aims to provide a comprehensive understanding of how Islam views and promotes social justice, and to explore the various dimensions of social justice in Islamic thought.

The book is divided into several chapters, each focusing on a specific aspect of social justice in Islam. We start by exploring the concept of justice in Islamic thought, and then delve into the Quranic perspective on social justice. We also examine the Prophetic tradition and its teachings on social justice, and discuss the principles of equality and equity in Islam.

Subsequent chapters of the book explore various aspects of social justice in Islam, including economic justice, political justice, gender justice, and environmental justice. We also discuss the role of Islamic jurisprudence and Islamic finance in promoting social justice, and examine contemporary issues and challenges related to social justice in Muslim communities and societies.

Throughout the book, we emphasize the importance of harmony and equity in achieving social justice. We argue that social justice in Islam is not just about ensuring fairness and equality, but also about fostering a sense of unity, compassion, and mutual respect among all members of society.

We hope that this book will serve as a valuable resource for students, scholars, and anyone interested in understanding how Islam views and promotes social justice. May Allah guide us and grant us the wisdom to uphold justice and equity in all our dealings.

1: Introduction to Social Justice in Islam

Social justice is a fundamental principle in Islam, deeply rooted in its teachings and practices. It is a concept that encompasses fairness, equality, and the establishment of a just society where every individual is treated with dignity and respect. In Islamic thought, social justice is not merely a theoretical ideal but a practical obligation that must be actively pursued and implemented in all aspects of life.

At the heart of Islamic teachings on social justice is the concept of 'Adl', which means justice and equity. The Quran emphasizes the importance of justice in numerous verses, stating that "God commands justice and fair dealing" (Quran 16:90) and "O you who have believed, be persistently standing firm in justice, witnesses for Allah, even if it be against yourselves or parents and relatives" (Quran 4:135). These verses underscore the principle that justice is not subjective or situational but an absolute standard that must be upheld under all circumstances.

The Prophet Muhammad (peace be upon him) also emphasized the importance of justice in his teachings and actions. He said, "The most beloved of people according to Allah is he who brings most benefit, and the most beloved of deeds according to Allah the Mighty, the Magnificent, is that you bring happiness to a fellow Muslim, or relieve him of distress, or pay off his debt, or stave away hunger from him. It is more beloved to me that I walk with my brother Muslim in his time of need than I stay secluded in the mosque for a month" (Al-Tabarani). This hadith highlights the importance of compassion, empathy, and solidarity in Islamic teachings on social justice.

In Islamic jurisprudence, the concept of social justice is manifested in various ways, including the obligation to pay zakat (charity) and the prohibition of usury (riba). Zakat is one of the five pillars of Islam and is a form of obligatory charity that aims to redistribute wealth from the rich to the poor, thereby ensuring a more equitable distribution of resources in society. The prohibition of usury is based on the principle that exploitation and unfair gain are contrary to the values of justice and equity.

In contemporary times, the concept of social justice in Islam has been applied to a wide range of issues, including poverty alleviation, gender equality, and environmental sustainability. Islamic scholars and activists have called for the implementation of Islamic principles of social justice in addressing these issues, emphasizing the importance of holistic and sustainable solutions that are grounded in Islamic teachings.

In conclusion, the concept of social justice in Islam is a central tenet of the faith, emphasizing the importance of justice, equity, and compassion in all aspects of life. It is a concept that is deeply rooted in Islamic teachings and practices, and it serves as a guiding principle for Muslims in their interactions with others and their efforts to create a more just and equitable society.

2: Concept of Justice in Islamic Thought

The concept of justice in Islamic thought is multifaceted, encompassing both divine justice and human justice. In Islamic theology, justice is considered one of the primary attributes of God, and it is believed that God's justice is perfect, absolute, and beyond human comprehension. Islamic teachings emphasize the importance of justice in all aspects of life, from personal conduct to social and political affairs.

At the core of the Islamic concept of justice is the belief that all human beings are equal in the sight of God and that they are entitled to fair and equal treatment under the law. This principle is enshrined in the Quran, which states, "O you who have believed, be persistently standing firm in justice, witnesses for Allah, even if it be against yourselves or parents and relatives" (Quran 4:135). This verse underscores the idea that justice is not only a duty towards others but also towards oneself, requiring individuals to uphold justice even when it may be against their own interests.

In Islamic jurisprudence, justice is seen as a fundamental objective of the Shariah, or Islamic law. The Shariah is based on the principles of justice, equality, and compassion, and it aims to create a just and equitable society where everyone's rights are respected and protected. Islamic jurists have developed a sophisticated legal framework to ensure that justice is served in all areas of life, including criminal law, family law, and commercial law.

One of the key principles of justice in Islamic thought is the concept of 'qist', which means fairness and balance. Islamic teachings emphasize the importance of striking a balance between competing interests and ensuring that no one is unjustly harmed or deprived of their rights. This principle is reflected in the Quranic injunction, "And do not consume one another's wealth unjustly or send it [in bribery] to the rulers in order that [they might aid] you [to] consume a portion of the wealth of the people in sin, while you know [it is unlawful]" (Quran 2:188).

In addition to divine justice, Islamic teachings also emphasize the importance of human justice, which is the responsibility of individuals, communities, and governments to uphold. The Prophet Muhammad (peace be upon him) said, "Help your brother, whether he is an oppressor or he is oppressed." The companions asked, "O Messenger of Allah, we help the oppressed, but how do we help an oppressor?" The Prophet said, "By preventing him from oppressing others" (Sahih Bukhari). This hadith highlights the importance of standing up against injustice and oppression, even if it means confronting those in positions of power.

In conclusion, the concept of justice in Islamic thought is a central tenet of the faith, emphasizing the importance of fairness, equality, and compassion in all aspects of life. It is a concept that is deeply rooted in Islamic teachings and practices, and it serves as a guiding principle for Muslims in their interactions with others and their efforts to create a more just and equitable society.

3: The Quranic Perspective on Social Justice

The Quran, as the holy book of Islam, provides a comprehensive framework for understanding and implementing social justice. It emphasizes the importance of justice in all aspects of life and provides guidance on how individuals, communities, and societies can achieve justice in their interactions. The Quranic perspective on social justice is based on several key principles, including fairness, equality, compassion, and accountability.

One of the central themes of the Quran is the concept of 'Adl', which means justice and equity. The Quran emphasizes that God is just and that His justice is absolute and perfect. It states, "God commands justice and fair dealing" (Quran 16:90) and "O you who have believed, be persistently standing firm in justice, witnesses for Allah, even if it be against yourselves or parents and relatives" (Quran 4:135). These verses underscore the importance of justice as a fundamental principle of Islam and emphasize the need for individuals to uphold justice even when it may be against their own interests.

The Quran also emphasizes the importance of equality in Islam. It states, "O mankind, indeed We have created you from male and female and made you peoples and tribes that you may know one another. Indeed, the most noble of you in the sight of Allah is the most righteous of you. Indeed, Allah is Knowing and Acquainted" (Quran 49:13). This verse highlights the equality of all human beings in the sight of God and emphasizes that the true measure of a person's worth is their piety and righteousness, not their race, ethnicity, or social status.

In addition to fairness and equality, the Quran also emphasizes compassion and empathy towards others. It states, "And the servants of the Most Merciful are those who walk upon the earth easily, and when the ignorant address them [harshly], they say [words of] peace" (Quran 25:63). This verse highlights the importance of responding to ignorance and hostility with kindness and compassion, and it emphasizes the need for individuals to treat others with respect and dignity, regardless of their circumstances.

The Quran also emphasizes the importance of accountability in Islam. It states, "And We have certainly created man, and We know what his soul whispers to him, and We are closer to him than [his] jugular vein" (Quran 50:16). This verse emphasizes that God is aware of all of our actions and intentions and that we will be held accountable for them in the Hereafter. This principle of accountability serves as a deterrent against injustice and wrongdoing and emphasizes the importance of acting justly and responsibly in all aspects of life.

In conclusion, the Quranic perspective on social justice is based on several key principles, including fairness, equality, compassion, and accountability. It emphasizes the importance of justice in all aspects of life and provides guidance on how individuals, communities, and societies can achieve justice in their interactions. Overall, the Quranic perspective on social justice is a comprehensive and holistic framework that emphasizes the importance of treating others with fairness, compassion, and respect, and it serves as a guide for Muslims in their efforts to create a more just and equitable society.

4: The Prophetic Tradition and Social Justice

The Prophetic tradition, or Sunnah, plays a crucial role in shaping the concept of social justice in Islam. Prophet Muhammad (peace be upon him) is considered the ideal example for Muslims to follow, and his teachings and actions provide guidance on how to establish and maintain social justice in society.

One of the key teachings of the Prophet Muhammad (peace be upon him) regarding social justice is the importance of fairness and equity in all dealings. He emphasized the need to treat all individuals, regardless of their background or status, with fairness and respect. The Prophet said, "Whoever has a favor done for him and says to the one who did it, 'JazakAllahu khayran,' has done enough to thank him" (Tirmidhi). This hadith highlights the importance of acknowledging and appreciating the efforts of others, regardless of their status or position in society.

The Prophet Muhammad (peace be upon him) also emphasized the importance of caring for the less fortunate members of society. He said, "The believer's shade on the Day of Resurrection will be his charity" (Al-Tirmidhi). This hadith highlights the importance of giving charity and caring for the poor and needy as a means of achieving social justice.

Another key aspect of the Prophetic tradition regarding social justice is the concept of accountability. The Prophet emphasized the importance of individuals being held accountable for their actions and encouraged his followers to speak out against injustice. He said, "Help your brother, whether he is an oppressor or he is oppressed." The companions asked, "O Messenger of Allah, we help the oppressed, but how do we help an oppressor?" The Prophet said, "By preventing him from oppressing others" (Sahih Bukhari). This hadith highlights the importance of standing up against injustice and oppression, even if it means confronting those in positions of power.

In addition to his teachings, the Prophet Muhammad (peace be upon him) also set an example through his actions. He was known for his honesty, integrity, and compassion towards others, regardless of their background or beliefs. His actions serve as a model for Muslims to follow in their efforts to establish social justice in society.

In conclusion, the Prophetic tradition plays a crucial role in shaping the concept of social justice in Islam. The teachings and actions of the Prophet Muhammad (peace be upon him) emphasize the importance of fairness, equity, compassion, and accountability in all aspects of life. Muslims are encouraged to follow the example of the Prophet in their efforts to establish a just and equitable society.

5: Equality and Equity in Islam

In Islamic teachings, the concepts of equality and equity are central to the understanding of social justice. While these terms are sometimes used interchangeably, they have distinct meanings in the context of Islamic thought.

Equality in Islam refers to the equal worth and dignity of all human beings in the sight of God. The Quran emphasizes the equality of all people, stating, "O mankind, indeed We have created you from male and female and made you peoples and tribes that you may know one another. Indeed, the most noble of you in the sight of Allah is the most righteous of you. Indeed, Allah is Knowing and Acquainted" (Quran 49:13). This verse highlights the idea that all human beings are equal in their humanity, regardless of their race, ethnicity, or social status.

Equity, on the other hand, refers to the fair distribution of resources and opportunities based on individual needs and circumstances. Islamic teachings emphasize the importance of equity in ensuring social justice. The Quran states, "And when you give your word, do so justly, even if a near relative is concerned; and fulfill your obligations before Allah. This He has enjoined upon you that you may remember" (Quran 6:152). This verse highlights the importance of fairness and equity in all dealings, even if it means going against one's own interests.

Islamic jurisprudence provides guidelines for achieving equity in various aspects of life. For example, in matters of inheritance, Islamic law stipulates that male and female heirs should receive their fair share of the deceased's estate, based on their relationship to the deceased and their needs. This ensures that everyone receives their due rights and that wealth is distributed fairly among family members.

In addition to material equity, Islam also emphasizes spiritual and moral equity. The Prophet Muhammad (peace be upon him) said, "The believers, in their love, mutual kindness, and close ties, are like one body; when any part complains, the whole body responds to it with wakefulness and fever" (Sahih Muslim). This hadith highlights the importance of caring for one another and ensuring that all members of society are treated with compassion and respect.

Overall, equality and equity are foundational principles in Islamic thought, emphasizing the equal worth and dignity of all human beings and the importance of fair and just treatment for everyone. These principles are central to the concept of social justice in Islam and serve as a guide for Muslims in their interactions with others and their efforts to create a more just and equitable society.

6: Economic Justice in Islamic Principles

Economic justice is a central theme in Islamic principles, which provide a framework for addressing economic issues such as wealth distribution, poverty alleviation, and fair trade practices. The teachings of Islam emphasize the importance of economic justice as a means of ensuring the well-being and welfare of all members of society, particularly the less fortunate.

One of the key principles of economic justice in Islam is the concept of wealth distribution. Islam recognizes that wealth is a trust from God and should be distributed fairly among all members of society. The Quran states, "And in their wealth there is acknowledged right for the needy and destitute" (Quran 51:19), highlighting the importance of giving to those in need and ensuring that wealth is not concentrated in the hands of a few.

Islamic teachings also emphasize the prohibition of usury (riba) and exploitation in economic transactions. The Quran prohibits usury, stating, "Those who consume interest cannot stand [on the Day of Resurrection] except as one stands who is being beaten by Satan into insanity" (Quran 2:275). This prohibition is aimed at preventing exploitation and ensuring that economic transactions are conducted fairly and ethically.

Another key principle of economic justice in Islam is the concept of zakat, or obligatory charity. Zakat is one of the five pillars of Islam and is a form of wealth redistribution that aims to alleviate poverty and ensure a more equitable distribution of wealth in society. The Quran states, "And establish prayer and give zakat, and whatever good you put forward for yourselves - you will find it with Allah. Indeed, Allah of what you do, is Seeing" (Quran 2:110), highlighting the importance of giving zakat as a means of seeking God's pleasure and blessings.

Islamic teachings also emphasize the importance of fair trade practices and ethical business conduct. The Prophet Muhammad (peace be upon him) said, "The seller and the buyer have the right to keep or return goods as long as they have not parted or till they part; and if both the parties spoke the truth and described the defects and qualities [of the goods], then they would be blessed in their transaction, and if they told lies or hid something, then the blessings of their transaction would be lost" (Sahih Bukhari). This hadith emphasizes the importance of honesty and transparency in business dealings and highlights the ethical principles that should govern economic transactions in Islam.

Overall, economic justice is a central theme in Islamic principles, which emphasize the importance of wealth distribution, fair trade practices, and ethical business conduct. These principles aim to ensure the well-being and welfare of all members of society and to create a more just and equitable economic system based on Islamic teachings.

7: Political Justice in Islamic Governance

Political justice in Islamic governance is a concept that is deeply rooted in the teachings of Islam, which emphasize the importance of justice, accountability, and good governance in all aspects of political life. Islamic teachings provide guidance on how political leaders should govern and how citizens should engage with their leaders to ensure justice and fairness in society.

One of the key principles of political justice in Islamic governance is the concept of 'Shura', or consultation. The Quran emphasizes the importance of consultation in decision-making, stating, "And those who have responded to their lord and established prayer and whose affair is [determined by] consultation among themselves, and from what We have provided them, they spend" (Quran 42:38). This verse highlights the importance of consultation in governance and emphasizes the need for political leaders to seek the advice and counsel of others in making decisions that affect the welfare of society.

Another key principle of political justice in Islamic governance is the concept of 'Amanah', or trust. Islamic teachings emphasize that political leaders are entrusted with power and authority by God and that they are accountable for their actions. The Prophet Muhammad (peace be upon him) said, "All of you are shepherds and each of you is responsible for his flock" (Sahih Bukhari). This hadith highlights the importance of political leaders being accountable to their constituents and ensuring that they govern with justice and fairness.

Islamic teachings also emphasize the importance of upholding the rule of law and ensuring that justice is accessible to all members of society. The Quran states, "O you who have believed, be persistently standing firm in justice, witnesses for Allah, even if it be against yourselves or parents and relatives. Whether one is rich or poor, Allah is more worthy of both" (Quran 4:135). This verse highlights the importance of upholding justice and fairness in all aspects of governance, regardless of one's social status or position in society.

In Islamic governance, political leaders are expected to govern with compassion, humility, and integrity, and to seek the well-being and welfare of all members of society. The Prophet Muhammad (peace be upon him) said, "The best of rulers are those whom you love and who love you, who pray for you and you pray for them. The worst of rulers are those whom you hate and who hate you, whom you curse and who curse you" (Muslim). This hadith emphasizes the importance of political leaders being just and fair in their governance and seeking the well-being of their constituents.

Overall, political justice in Islamic governance is a concept that emphasizes the importance of justice, accountability, and good governance in ensuring the well-being and welfare of all members of society. It is a concept that is deeply rooted in Islamic teachings and provides a framework for political leaders and citizens to govern and engage with one another in a just and equitable manner.

8: Social Welfare and Charity in Islam

Social welfare and charity are central concepts in Islam, emphasizing the importance of caring for the less fortunate members of society and ensuring their well-being and welfare. Islamic teachings encourage Muslims to be charitable and compassionate towards others, particularly those in need, and provide guidance on how to practice charity in a way that is beneficial and impactful.

One of the key principles of social welfare and charity in Islam is the concept of 'Zakat', or obligatory charity. Zakat is one of the five pillars of Islam and is a form of wealth redistribution that aims to alleviate poverty and ensure a more equitable distribution of wealth in society. The Quran states, "And establish prayer and give zakat, and whatever good you put forward for yourselves - you will find it with Allah. Indeed, Allah of what you do, is Seeing" (Quran 2:110), highlighting the importance of giving zakat as a means of seeking God's pleasure and blessings.

In addition to zakat, Islam emphasizes the importance of voluntary charity, known as 'Sadaqah'. The Prophet Muhammad (peace be upon him) said, "Charity does not decrease wealth" (Muslim), emphasizing the importance of giving in charity as a means of earning reward from God and purifying one's wealth. Sadaqah can take many forms, including giving money, food, or other resources to those in need, and Islam encourages Muslims to be generous in their giving.

Islamic teachings also emphasize the importance of caring for specific categories of people who are in need, including orphans, widows, and the poor. The Quran states, "And they ask you about orphans. Say, 'Improvement for them is best. And if you mix your affairs with theirs - they are your brothers. And Allah knows the corrupter from the amender. And if Allah had willed, He could have put you in difficulty. Indeed, Allah is Exalted in Might and Wise'" (Quran 2:220), highlighting the importance of caring for orphans and ensuring their well-being and welfare.

In addition to individual acts of charity, Islam also emphasizes the importance of collective efforts to address social welfare issues. Islamic teachings encourage Muslims to work together to establish charitable organizations and initiatives that can provide long-term solutions to social welfare issues and ensure the well-being of all members of society.

Overall, social welfare and charity are central concepts in Islam, emphasizing the importance of caring for the less fortunate members of society and ensuring their well-being and welfare. Islam provides a comprehensive framework for practicing charity in a way that is beneficial and impactful, and encourages Muslims to be generous and compassionate towards others in need.

9: Human Rights in Islamic Law

Human rights in Islamic law are based on the Quran, the teachings of the Prophet Muhammad (peace be upon him), and the principles of Islamic jurisprudence. Islam emphasizes the importance of human dignity, equality, and justice, and provides a framework for protecting and promoting human rights in all aspects of life.

One of the key principles of human rights in Islamic law is the concept of 'Hifz al-Nafs', or the protection of life. Islam considers human life to be sacred and prohibits the taking of innocent life. The Quran states, "And do not kill the soul which Allah has forbidden, except by right" (Quran 17:33), emphasizing the sanctity of human life and the importance of protecting it from harm.

In addition to the protection of life, Islam also emphasizes the importance of preserving other human rights, including the right to freedom, justice, and dignity. The Quran states, "O you who have believed, be persistently standing firm for Allah, witnesses in justice, and do not let the hatred of a people prevent you from being just. Be just; that is nearer to righteousness. And fear Allah; indeed, Allah is Acquainted with what you do" (Quran 5:8), highlighting the importance of justice and fairness in all dealings.

Islamic teachings also emphasize the importance of upholding the rights of minorities and protecting them from discrimination and oppression. The Prophet Muhammad (peace be upon him) said, "Whoever wrongs a non-Muslim citizen of a Muslim state, or imposes on him a work he is unable to do, or deprives him of his rights, or takes something from him by force, I am his adversary on the Day of Judgment" (Abu Dawood). This hadith emphasizes the importance of treating all individuals, regardless of their faith or background, with respect and dignity.

In addition to these principles, Islamic law also provides specific rights for women, children, and other vulnerable groups in society. For example, Islam guarantees women the right to education, work, and property ownership, and prohibits any form of discrimination or violence against them. Similarly, Islam emphasizes the importance of protecting the rights of children and ensuring their well-being and welfare.

Overall, human rights in Islamic law are based on the principles of justice, equality, and compassion, and emphasize the importance of protecting and promoting the rights of all individuals, regardless of their background or beliefs. Islam provides a comprehensive framework for addressing human rights issues and ensuring the well-being and welfare of all members of society.

10: Gender Justice in Islam

Gender justice in Islam is a concept that emphasizes the equality, dignity, and rights of men and women in all aspects of life. Islamic teachings emphasize the importance of gender justice and provide guidance on how to achieve it through the implementation of Islamic principles and values.

One of the key principles of gender justice in Islam is the concept of 'Qiwamah', which refers to the responsibility of men to provide for and protect their families. While Qiwamah is often interpreted as implying male authority, Islamic scholars emphasize that it should be understood in the context of mutual respect and cooperation between men and women. The Quran states, "Men are the protectors and maintainers of women, because Allah has given the one more [strength] than the other, and because they support them from their means" (Quran 4:34), highlighting the complementary roles of men and women in society.

Islamic teachings also emphasize the importance of equality between men and women in the sight of God. The Quran states, "And their Lord responded to them, 'Never will I allow to be lost the work of [any] worker among you, whether male or female; you are of one another'" (Quran 3:195), emphasizing that both men and women are equal in their ability to earn reward from God through their actions.

In addition to these principles, Islam provides specific rights and protections for women in various aspects of life. For example, Islam guarantees women the right to education, work, and property ownership, and prohibits any form of discrimination or violence against them. The Prophet Muhammad (peace be upon him) said, "The best of you are those who are best to their wives" (Tirmidhi), emphasizing the importance of treating women with kindness, respect, and dignity.

Islamic teachings also emphasize the importance of women's participation in decision-making and public life. The Quran states, "The believing men and believing women are allies of one another. They enjoin what is right and forbid what is wrong" (Quran 9:71), highlighting the importance of cooperation and collaboration between men and women in promoting justice and righteousness in society.

Overall, gender justice in Islam is based on the principles of equality, dignity, and mutual respect between men and women. Islam provides a comprehensive framework for addressing gender issues and ensuring the well-being and welfare of both men and women in society.

11: Justice in Family and Relationships

Justice in family and relationships is a fundamental concept in Islam, emphasizing fairness, compassion, and respect in all dealings between family members and in relationships. Islamic teachings provide guidance on how to maintain justice in family life and emphasize the importance of mutual rights and responsibilities.

One of the key principles of justice in family and relationships in Islam is the concept of 'Adl', or fairness. The Quran emphasizes the importance of treating all family members with fairness and kindness, stating, "And give the women [upon marriage] their [bridal] gifts graciously. But if they give up willingly to you anything of it, then take it in satisfaction and ease" (Quran 4:4). This verse highlights the importance of fairness in marital relationships and emphasizes the need for husbands to treat their wives with kindness and generosity.

Islamic teachings also emphasize the importance of mutual respect and cooperation between spouses. The Prophet Muhammad (peace be upon him) said, "The best of you is the one who is best to his wife" (Tirmidhi), emphasizing the importance of treating one's spouse with kindness, respect, and dignity. Islam also emphasizes the importance of communication and resolving conflicts in a peaceful and respectful manner.

In addition to marital relationships, Islam also emphasizes the importance of justice in relationships between parents and children. The Quran states, "And We have enjoined upon man [care] for his parents. His mother carried him, [increasing her] in weakness upon weakness, and his weaning is in two years. Be grateful to Me and to your parents; to Me is the [final] destination" (Quran 31:14), highlighting the importance of honoring and respecting parents and fulfilling their rights.

Islamic teachings also emphasize the importance of justice in relationships with other family members, such as siblings and relatives. The Quran states, "O you who have believed, be persistently standing firm in justice, witnesses for Allah, even if it be against yourselves or parents and relatives. Whether one is rich or poor, Allah is more worthy of both" (Quran 4:135), emphasizing the importance of upholding justice and fairness in all family relationships.

Overall, justice in family and relationships is a central concept in Islam, emphasizing the importance of fairness, compassion, and respect in all dealings between family members and in relationships. Islam provides a comprehensive framework for maintaining justice in family life and emphasizes the importance of mutual rights and responsibilities in ensuring the well-being and welfare of all family members.

12: Environmental Justice in Islamic Ethics

Environmental justice in Islamic ethics emphasizes the responsibility of humans to be stewards of the Earth and to protect and preserve the environment for future generations. Islamic teachings emphasize the importance of maintaining a balance and harmony in the natural world and provide guidance on how to achieve environmental justice through ethical and sustainable practices.

One of the key principles of environmental justice in Islamic ethics is the concept of 'Khalifah', or stewardship. The Quran states, "It is He who has made you successors (khalifah) upon the earth..." (Quran 35:39), emphasizing that humans are stewards of the Earth and have a responsibility to care for and protect it. This concept is further reinforced by the Prophet Muhammad (peace be upon him), who said, "The world is beautiful and verdant, and verily God, be He exalted, has made you His stewards in it, and He sees how you acquit yourselves" (Muslim).

Islamic teachings also emphasize the importance of conservation and sustainable use of natural resources. The Quran states, "Eat and drink from the provision of Allah, and do not commit abuse on the earth, spreading corruption" (Quran 2:60), highlighting the importance of using resources wisely and avoiding wastefulness. The Prophet Muhammad (peace be upon him) also emphasized the importance of conservation, saying, "If any Muslim plants a tree or sows a field, and a human, bird or animal eats from it, it shall be reckoned as charity from him" (Bukhari).

In addition to conservation, Islamic ethics also emphasize the importance of justice in environmental matters. The Quran states, "Do not pollute the earth after it has been set in order..." (Quran 7:56), highlighting the importance of protecting the environment from pollution and degradation. Islamic teachings also emphasize the rights of animals and the importance of treating them with kindness and compassion. The Prophet Muhammad (peace be upon him) said, "Whoever is kind to the creatures of God, he is kind to himself" (Bukhari).

Overall, environmental justice in Islamic ethics emphasizes the importance of stewardship, conservation, and justice in all interactions with the environment. Islam provides a comprehensive framework for achieving environmental justice through ethical and sustainable practices, emphasizing the importance of protecting and preserving the environment for future generations.

13: Islamic Jurisprudence and Social Justice

Islamic jurisprudence, also known as fiqh, plays a crucial role in promoting social justice in Islamic societies. Fiqh is the human understanding and interpretation of Islamic law based on the Quran, the teachings of the Prophet Muhammad (peace be upon him), and the consensus of Islamic scholars. Islamic jurisprudence provides a framework for addressing social issues and ensuring justice and equity in all aspects of life.

One of the key principles of Islamic jurisprudence that promotes social justice is the concept of 'Maqasid al-Shariah', or the objectives of Islamic law. Maqasid al-Shariah emphasizes the overarching goals of Islamic law, which include the preservation of life, religion, intellect, progeny, and property. Islamic jurists use these objectives as a guide for interpreting and applying Islamic law in a way that promotes justice and serves the common good.

Islamic jurisprudence also emphasizes the importance of upholding justice and fairness in all aspects of life. The Quran states, "Indeed, Allah commands justice and good conduct and giving to relatives and forbids immorality and bad conduct and oppression. He admonishes you that perhaps you will be reminded" (Quran 16:90), highlighting the importance of justice as a fundamental principle of Islam. Islamic law provides guidelines for ensuring justice in various aspects of life, including criminal law, family law, and economic transactions.

In addition to promoting justice, Islamic jurisprudence also emphasizes the importance of compassion and mercy in social relations. The Prophet Muhammad (peace be upon him) said, "Whoever shows no mercy, will not be shown mercy" (Bukhari), emphasizing the importance of treating others with kindness and compassion. Islamic law provides guidelines for resolving disputes and conflicts in a way that promotes reconciliation and peace.

Overall, Islamic jurisprudence plays a crucial role in promoting social justice in Islamic societies. It provides a framework for addressing social issues and ensuring justice and equity in all aspects of life. Islamic jurists use the principles of Islamic law to interpret and apply Islamic teachings in a way that promotes justice, compassion, and mercy in society.

14: Islamic Finance and Social Justice

Islamic finance is based on principles that promote social justice and economic stability. It emphasizes ethical and equitable financial transactions that benefit society as a whole. Islamic finance is guided by Shariah, the Islamic law derived from the Quran and the teachings of the Prophet Muhammad (peace be upon him), which prohibits certain practices such as interest (riba) and promotes risk-sharing and asset backing.

One of the key principles of Islamic finance that promotes social justice is the prohibition of riba, or interest. Islamic finance emphasizes the importance of fair and equitable transactions that do not exploit or harm individuals. The Quran states, "Those who consume interest cannot stand [on the Day of Resurrection] except as one stands who is being beaten by Satan into insanity" (Quran 2:275), highlighting the serious nature of engaging in interest-based transactions.

Instead of interest, Islamic finance promotes profit-sharing and risk-sharing arrangements, such as mudarabah (profit-sharing) and musharakah (partnership), where profits and losses are shared between the parties involved. These arrangements promote economic justice by ensuring that both parties share in the risks and rewards of the investment.

Islamic finance also emphasizes the importance of ethical investment and prohibits investments in businesses that are considered harmful or unethical, such as those involved in gambling, alcohol, or pork. This promotes social justice by encouraging investment in businesses that benefit society and adhere to ethical standards.

Another key principle of Islamic finance that promotes social justice is the concept of zakat, or obligatory charity. Islamic finance requires Muslims to pay a portion of their wealth to the poor and needy, which helps to reduce poverty and inequality in society. Zakat is seen as a means of redistributing wealth and ensuring that everyone has access to the basic necessities of life.

Overall, Islamic finance promotes social justice by emphasizing fair and equitable financial transactions, ethical investment, and the redistribution of wealth through zakat. It provides a framework for financial transactions that benefit society as a whole and adhere to ethical and moral principles.

15: Islamophobia and Social Justice

Islamophobia refers to the irrational fear, prejudice, and discrimination against Islam and Muslims. It manifests in various forms, including verbal abuse, physical attacks, stereotypes, and negative portrayals in media and politics. Islamophobia undermines social justice by perpetuating stereotypes, promoting discrimination, and hindering the full participation of Muslims in society.

One of the key issues with Islamophobia is its impact on the rights and freedoms of Muslims. Muslims may face discrimination in employment, education, housing, and other areas of life due to Islamophobic attitudes and beliefs. This undermines social justice by denying Muslims the same opportunities and rights as others in society.

Islamophobia also contributes to the marginalization and alienation of Muslims, leading to social exclusion and isolation. This can have negative impacts on the mental health and well-being of Muslims, as well as their sense of belonging and identity within society.

Another aspect of Islamophobia is its impact on community cohesion and social harmony. Islamophobic attitudes can create divisions within society and contribute to tensions between different communities. This undermines social justice by eroding trust and understanding between people of different backgrounds and beliefs.

Combatting Islamophobia requires a multi-faceted approach that addresses its root causes and promotes understanding and respect for diversity. This includes education and awareness-raising efforts to challenge stereotypes and misinformation about Islam and Muslims. It also involves promoting interfaith dialogue and collaboration to build bridges between different communities and foster mutual respect and understanding.

Overall, Islamophobia undermines social justice by perpetuating discrimination, promoting division, and denying Muslims the same rights and opportunities as others in society. Combatting Islamophobia is essential for promoting a more just and inclusive society where all individuals are treated with dignity and respect, regardless of their religion or background.

16: Colonialism and its Impact on Social Justice in Muslim Societies

Colonialism refers to the establishment, maintenance, acquisition, and expansion of colonies in one territory by people from another territory. The impact of colonialism on social justice in Muslim societies has been profound and far-reaching, affecting various aspects of life including political, economic, social, and cultural spheres.

One of the key impacts of colonialism on social justice in Muslim societies was the imposition of foreign political systems and governance structures. Colonial powers often established authoritarian and exploitative systems of governance that marginalized indigenous populations and undermined their rights and freedoms. This led to widespread inequality and injustice in many Muslim societies.

Colonialism also had a significant impact on the economic development of Muslim societies. Colonial powers often exploited the natural resources and labor of colonized territories for their own benefit, leading to economic exploitation and underdevelopment. This resulted in widespread poverty and inequality in many Muslim societies, which continue to have lasting effects to this day.

Furthermore, colonialism had a profound impact on the social and cultural fabric of Muslim societies. Colonial powers often imposed their own cultural norms and values on colonized populations, leading to the erosion of indigenous cultures and traditions. This led to a loss of identity and cultural heritage for many Muslim communities, which continue to struggle with issues of cultural preservation and identity.

In addition, colonialism had a lasting impact on the political landscape of many Muslim societies. Colonial powers often divided and fragmented colonized territories along artificial lines, leading to the creation of modern nation-states that were often ethnically and culturally diverse. This has contributed to ongoing conflicts and tensions in many Muslim societies, as different groups vie for power and resources within these artificial borders.

Overall, colonialism has had a profound and lasting impact on social justice in Muslim societies. It has led to widespread inequality, exploitation, and marginalization of indigenous populations, and has contributed to ongoing issues of poverty, conflict, and cultural identity. Addressing the legacy of colonialism is essential for promoting social justice and equality in Muslim societies, and requires a comprehensive approach that addresses the root causes and effects of colonialism on all aspects of society.

17: Modern Challenges to Social Justice in Islamic Context

Modern challenges to social justice in an Islamic context are multifaceted and diverse, reflecting the complex social, economic, and political realities faced by Muslim societies around the world. These challenges are often exacerbated by factors such as poverty, corruption, conflict, and discrimination, which can hinder the achievement of social justice and equality for all members of society.

One of the key modern challenges to social justice in Islamic contexts is economic inequality. Many Muslim-majority countries struggle with high levels of poverty and income inequality, which can lead to social unrest and instability. Economic inequality is often exacerbated by factors such as corruption, lack of access to education and healthcare, and uneven distribution of resources.

Another major challenge to social justice in Islamic contexts is political instability and conflict. Many Muslim-majority countries have experienced political turmoil, civil unrest, and armed conflict, which can have devastating consequences for social justice and human rights. Conflict and instability can lead to displacement, loss of life, and widespread human suffering, undermining efforts to achieve social justice and equality.

Discrimination and marginalization of minority groups are also significant challenges to social justice in Islamic contexts. Minority groups, including religious and ethnic minorities, often face discrimination, exclusion, and violence, which can hinder their ability to fully participate in society and access their rights. Addressing discrimination and promoting inclusion are essential for achieving social justice for all members of society.

Gender inequality is another major challenge to social justice in Islamic contexts. While Islam emphasizes the equality of men and women, many Muslim-majority countries struggle with gender-based discrimination and violence. Women often face barriers to education, employment, and political participation, limiting their ability to fully participate in society and access their rights.

Addressing these modern challenges to social justice in Islamic contexts requires a comprehensive approach that addresses the root causes of inequality and injustice. This includes promoting good governance, rule of law, and respect for human rights, as well as addressing economic disparities, conflict, discrimination, and gender inequality. By addressing these challenges, Muslim societies can work towards achieving social justice and equality for all members of society, in line with Islamic teachings and principles.

18: Globalization and Social Justice in Islam

Globalization has had a significant impact on social justice in Islamic contexts, presenting both opportunities and challenges for Muslim societies. Globalization refers to the increasing interconnectedness of the world through the exchange of goods, services, ideas, and cultures across borders. While globalization has led to economic growth and development in many parts of the world, it has also contributed to social inequalities and challenges in Islamic contexts.

One of the key challenges of globalization for social justice in Islamic contexts is economic inequality. Globalization has led to the expansion of global markets and increased economic interdependence, but it has also widened the gap between the rich and the poor within and between countries. Many Muslim-majority countries have struggled to benefit from globalization, leading to increased poverty, unemployment, and social unrest.

Globalization has also had a cultural impact on Islamic societies, leading to the spread of Western cultural values and practices. This has raised concerns among some Muslims about the erosion of traditional cultural values and the influence of Western ideologies. This cultural globalization has also led to challenges related to identity and social cohesion in Islamic societies.

On the other hand, globalization has also presented opportunities for social justice in Islamic contexts. It has facilitated the exchange of ideas and information, leading to greater awareness of social justice issues and the promotion of human rights. Globalization has also provided new avenues for economic development and empowerment, particularly through the expansion of technology and communication networks.

Islamic teachings emphasize the importance of social justice and equitable distribution of resources. The Quran states, "And do not consume one another's wealth unjustly or send it [in bribery] to the rulers in order that [they might aid] you [to] consume a portion of the wealth of the people in sin, while you know [it is unlawful]" (Quran 2:188). This verse highlights the importance of fairness and justice in economic transactions, which can be applied to the challenges posed by globalization.

Overall, globalization presents both opportunities and challenges for social justice in Islamic contexts. By addressing the economic, cultural, and social implications of globalization, Muslim societies can work towards achieving social justice and equality for all members of society, in line with Islamic teachings and principles.

19: Islamic Movements for Social Justice

Islamic movements for social justice are diverse and dynamic, encompassing a wide range of groups and organizations that seek to promote social justice and equality in accordance with Islamic principles and values. These movements often emerge in response to perceived injustices and inequalities in society and aim to address these issues through various means, including advocacy, activism, and community organizing.

One of the key features of Islamic movements for social justice is their emphasis on the principles of justice, compassion, and equality found in Islamic teachings. These movements draw inspiration from the Quran and the teachings of the Prophet Muhammad (peace be upon him), which emphasize the importance of upholding the rights of the poor, the oppressed, and the marginalized in society.

Islamic movements for social justice often focus on a wide range of issues, including poverty alleviation, human rights, gender equality, and environmental protection. These movements work to raise awareness about these issues within Muslim communities and to mobilize support for positive change.

One example of an Islamic movement for social justice is the Islamic Renaissance Party of Tajikistan (IRPT), which emerged in the early 1990s following the collapse of the Soviet Union. The IRPT advocated for democratic reforms, social justice, and the rights of Muslims in Tajikistan. Despite facing persecution and repression from the Tajik government, the IRPT continued to work towards its goals of social justice and democracy.

Another example is the Muslim Brotherhood, which was founded in Egypt in 1928 and has since become one of the most influential Islamic movements in the world. The Muslim Brotherhood seeks to promote social justice and Islamic values through peaceful means, including social welfare programs, education, and community development initiatives.

Islamic movements for social justice often face challenges and obstacles in their work, including government repression, lack of resources, and opposition from conservative elements within Muslim societies. However, these movements continue to play a crucial role in advocating for social justice and equality in Islamic contexts, and their work has had a significant impact on Muslim communities around the world.

20: The Role of Islamic Institutions in Promoting Social Justice

Islamic institutions play a crucial role in promoting social justice in Muslim societies by upholding Islamic values and principles, providing services to the community, and advocating for positive change. These institutions include mosques, Islamic schools, charitable organizations, and religious scholars, among others. They work to address a wide range of social issues, including poverty, inequality, education, and healthcare, and play a key role in shaping the social and moral fabric of Muslim communities.

One of the key roles of Islamic institutions in promoting social justice is providing social welfare services to the community. Islamic teachings emphasize the importance of caring for the poor, the needy, and the marginalized, and Islamic institutions often provide services such as food aid, healthcare, and education to those in need. These services help to alleviate poverty and inequality in Muslim societies and ensure that all members of the community have access to basic necessities.

Islamic institutions also play a key role in advocating for social justice and human rights. Islamic scholars and leaders often speak out against injustice and oppression, and Islamic organizations work to raise awareness about social issues and advocate for positive change. For example, many Islamic organizations are involved in campaigns to end poverty, promote gender equality, and protect the environment.

In addition to providing services and advocacy, Islamic institutions also play a crucial role in educating the community about Islamic values and principles related to social justice. Islamic schools and mosques often teach about the importance of compassion, justice, and equality in Islam, and encourage community members to uphold these values in their daily lives. By educating the community about these principles, Islamic institutions help to foster a sense of social responsibility and solidarity among Muslims.

Overall, Islamic institutions play a crucial role in promoting social justice in Muslim societies. Through their work in providing services, advocating for positive change, and educating the community, these institutions help to uphold Islamic values and principles and ensure that all members of the community have access to justice, equality, and dignity.

21: Case Studies of Social Justice in Islamic History

Islamic history is replete with examples of social justice initiatives that have had a lasting impact on Muslim societies and beyond. These case studies highlight the application of Islamic principles to address social issues and promote equality and justice. Here are a few notable examples:

A: Caliph Umar ibn al-Khattab's Social Welfare Policies: During his reign as the second Caliph, Umar ibn al-Khattab implemented various social welfare policies to ensure the well-being of all citizens. He established a system of public treasury (Bait al-Mal) to provide financial support to the poor, orphans, and widows. Umar also appointed officials (Muhtasib) to monitor markets and ensure fair trade practices, demonstrating a commitment to economic justice.

B: The Foundation of the Bayt al-Mal in Medina: After the migration of the Prophet Muhammad (peace be upon him) and his followers to Medina, the Prophet established the Bayt al-Mal, or the public treasury. The Bayt al-Mal was used to support the poor, the needy, and those in debt, demonstrating a commitment to social welfare and economic justice.

C: The Social Reforms of Sultan Salahuddin Ayyubi: Salahuddin Ayyubi, known in the West as Saladin, was a renowned Muslim leader who recaptured Jerusalem from the Crusaders in 1187. Salahuddin implemented various social reforms, including the establishment of hospitals, schools, and soup kitchens to support the poor and vulnerable in society. He also promoted religious tolerance and respect for other faiths, demonstrating a commitment to social justice and equality.

D: The Ottoman Empire's Legal System: The Ottoman Empire, which spanned several centuries, implemented a legal system based on Islamic principles that promoted social justice and equality. The Ottoman legal system included provisions for the protection of minority rights, the establishment of charitable endowments (waqf), and the regulation of trade to ensure fair practices.

E: The Fatimid Caliphate's Educational Initiatives: The Fatimid Caliphate, which ruled parts of North Africa and the Middle East in the 10th to 12th centuries, was known for its emphasis on education and knowledge. The Fatimids established numerous educational institutions, including the University of Al-Qarawiyyin in Fez, Morocco, which is considered the oldest continuously operating university in the world. These educational initiatives promoted social mobility and access to knowledge, contributing to social justice and equality.

These case studies demonstrate how Islamic principles have been applied throughout history to promote social justice, economic equality, and the well-being of all members of society. They serve as a testament to the enduring relevance of Islamic teachings in addressing contemporary social issues and promoting a more just and equitable society.

22: Contemporary Issues of Social Justice in Muslim-majority Countries

Contemporary Muslim-majority countries face a range of social justice issues that impact the well-being and rights of their populations. These issues are often complex and multifaceted, stemming from a variety of factors including political instability, economic challenges, and social norms. Some of the key contemporary issues of social justice in Muslim-majority countries include:

A: Political Repression and Human Rights Violations: Many Muslim-majority countries experience political repression and human rights violations, including restrictions on freedom of speech, assembly, and association. Political dissent is often met with harsh crackdowns, leading to a lack of political freedoms and justice for citizens.

B: Economic Inequality and Poverty: Economic inequality is a significant issue in many Muslim-majority countries, with large disparities in wealth distribution. Poverty rates are often high, particularly in rural areas and among marginalized communities, leading to a lack of access to basic services such as healthcare, education, and housing.

C: Gender Inequality: Gender inequality remains a pervasive issue in many Muslim-majority countries, with women often facing discrimination in areas such as education, employment, and political participation. Laws and social norms that restrict women's rights and freedoms contribute to gender-based inequalities.

D: Corruption and Lack of Accountability: Corruption is a major challenge in many Muslim-majority countries, with high levels of corruption in government institutions and the private sector. This lack of accountability undermines social justice by perpetuating inequality and hindering development.

E: Violent Extremism and Terrorism: Some Muslim-majority countries face challenges related to violent extremism and terrorism, which pose serious threats to social stability and security. These issues can be exacerbated by political and economic grievances, as well as by the influence of extremist ideologies.

F: Environmental Degradation: Environmental degradation is a growing concern in many Muslim-majority countries, with issues such as deforestation, water scarcity, and air pollution posing serious threats to public health and well-being. Addressing these environmental challenges is crucial for promoting social justice and sustainable development.

Addressing these contemporary issues of social justice in Muslim-majority countries requires a comprehensive approach that addresses the root causes of inequality and injustice. This includes promoting good governance, accountability, and transparency, as well as addressing economic disparities, gender inequality, and environmental degradation. By addressing these challenges, Muslim-majority countries can work towards promoting social justice and improving the well-being of all their citizens.

23: Interfaith and Inter-cultural Dialogue for Social Justice

Interfaith and intercultural dialogue play a crucial role in promoting social justice by fostering understanding, respect, and cooperation among different religious and cultural communities. These dialogues provide opportunities for people of different backgrounds to come together, share their perspectives, and work towards common goals, including promoting social justice and addressing shared challenges.

One of the key ways in which interfaith and intercultural dialogue promote social justice is by challenging stereotypes and prejudices. By engaging in dialogue, individuals can learn about the beliefs, practices, and values of others, helping to dispel misconceptions and promote mutual respect. This can help to reduce discrimination and promote inclusivity in society.

Interfaith and intercultural dialogue also promote social justice by building bridges between communities and fostering cooperation. Through dialogue, individuals and communities can identify common values and goals, and work together to address issues such as poverty, inequality, and discrimination. This can lead to more inclusive and equitable societies where all members feel valued and respected.

Furthermore, interfaith and intercultural dialogue can help to promote peace and conflict resolution. By bringing together people of different backgrounds, dialogue can help to build understanding and empathy, reducing the likelihood of conflict and promoting peaceful coexistence.

This is particularly important in regions where religious or cultural differences have been sources of tension and conflict.

In conclusion, interfaith and intercultural dialogue are powerful tools for promoting social justice and building more inclusive and peaceful societies. By promoting understanding, respect, and cooperation among different religious and cultural communities, these dialogues help to challenge stereotypes, reduce discrimination, and promote peace and harmony.

24: Humanitarian Aid and Social Justice in Islam

Humanitarian aid plays a vital role in promoting social justice in Islam by upholding the principles of compassion, solidarity, and equality. Islamic teachings emphasize the importance of helping those in need and providing support to the less fortunate members of society. Humanitarian aid in Islam encompasses a wide range of activities, including providing food, shelter, healthcare, and education to those in need, as well as promoting social justice and human rights.

One of the key principles of humanitarian aid in Islam is the concept of 'Zakat', or obligatory charity. Zakat is one of the five pillars of Islam and requires Muslims to donate a portion of their wealth to the poor and needy. Zakat is seen as a means of redistributing wealth and ensuring that everyone has access to the basic necessities of life. By fulfilling their duty of Zakat, Muslims contribute to social justice by helping to alleviate poverty and inequality in society.

In addition to Zakat, Islam also emphasizes the importance of voluntary charity, or 'Sadaqah'. Sadaqah can take many forms, including providing financial assistance, volunteering time and skills, and offering emotional support to those in need. By engaging in Sadaqah, Muslims can further contribute to social justice by supporting the most vulnerable members of society and promoting a culture of compassion and generosity.

Islamic teachings also emphasize the importance of providing humanitarian aid without discrimination or prejudice. The Prophet Muhammad (peace be upon him) said, "All creatures are the dependents of Allah, and the most beloved of them to Allah is he who is kind to His dependents" (Al-Adab al-Mufrad). This emphasizes the importance of treating all people with kindness and compassion, regardless of their background or beliefs.

Overall, humanitarian aid plays a crucial role in promoting social justice in Islam by upholding the principles of compassion, solidarity, and equality. By fulfilling their obligations of Zakat and engaging in voluntary charity, Muslims can contribute to a more just and equitable society where all members have access to the basic necessities of life and are treated with dignity and respect.

25: Education and Social Justice in Islamic Perspective

Education plays a crucial role in promoting social justice in Islam by empowering individuals, promoting equality, and fostering a culture of knowledge and enlightenment. Islamic teachings emphasize the importance of education as a means of uplifting society and ensuring that all members have access to opportunities for personal and intellectual growth.

One of the key principles of education in Islam is the concept of 'ilm', or knowledge. The Quran emphasizes the importance of seeking knowledge and understanding, stating, "Read! In the name of your Lord who created. Created man from a clot. Read! And your Lord is the Most Generous. Who taught by the pen. Taught man that which he knew not" (Quran 96:1-5). This verse highlights the importance of education as a means of acquiring knowledge and understanding the world around us.

Islamic teachings also emphasize the importance of education for both men and women. The Prophet Muhammad (peace be upon him) said, "Seeking knowledge is obligatory upon every Muslim" (Ibn Majah). This hadith highlights the importance of education for all members of society, regardless of gender, and underscores the value of knowledge in Islam.

Education in Islam is not just about acquiring academic knowledge, but also about cultivating moral and ethical values. Islamic education emphasizes the importance of character development, compassion, and social responsibility. The Prophet Muhammad (peace be upon him) said, "I have only been sent to perfect good character" (Al-Adab al-Mufrad). This emphasizes the importance of education in shaping individuals who are not only knowledgeable but also morally upright and socially responsible.

In addition to promoting individual empowerment, education in Islam also plays a crucial role in promoting social justice and equality. By providing all members of society with access to quality education, Islam seeks to ensure that everyone has the opportunity to fulfill their potential and contribute to the betterment of society. Education helps to break the cycle of poverty and inequality by providing individuals with the skills and knowledge they need to improve their lives and the lives of others.

Overall, education plays a crucial role in promoting social justice in Islam by empowering individuals, promoting equality, and fostering a culture of knowledge and enlightenment. By emphasizing the importance of education for all members of society and cultivating moral and ethical values, Islam seeks to create a more just and equitable society where everyone has the opportunity to thrive.

26: Media and Social Justice in Islam

Media plays a crucial role in promoting social justice in Islam by shaping public opinion, raising awareness about social issues, and advocating for positive change. Islamic teachings emphasize the importance of using media responsibly and ethically to promote justice, fairness, and compassion in society.

One of the key principles of media in Islam is the concept of 'Sadaqah al-Fitr', or truthful speech. The Quran emphasizes the importance of speaking the truth and avoiding falsehood, stating, "O you who have believed, fear Allah and speak words of appropriate justice" (Quran 33:70). This principle highlights the importance of using media to convey accurate information and promote understanding and justice.

Islamic teachings also emphasize the importance of using media to promote social cohesion and unity. The Prophet Muhammad (peace be upon him) said, "The believers in their mutual kindness, compassion, and sympathy are just like one body. When any part of the body suffers, the whole body feels pain" (Sahih Bukhari). This hadith emphasizes the importance of using media to promote empathy and solidarity among members of society.

Media in Islam is also expected to promote social justice by advocating for the rights of the oppressed and marginalized. The Quran emphasizes the importance of standing up for justice, stating, "O you who have believed, be persistently standing firm in justice, witnesses for Allah, even if it be against yourselves or parents and relatives"

(Quran 4:135). This principle highlights the importance of using media to advocate for the rights of those who are oppressed or marginalized in society.

In addition to promoting social justice, media in Islam is also expected to promote moral and ethical values. The Quran emphasizes the importance of promoting virtue and preventing vice, stating, "And let there be [arising] from you a nation inviting to [all that is] good, enjoining what is right and forbidding what is wrong, and those will be the successful" (Quran 3:104). This principle highlights the importance of using media to promote moral and ethical values that contribute to a just and harmonious society.

Overall, media plays a crucial role in promoting social justice in Islam by shaping public opinion, raising awareness about social issues, and advocating for positive change. By adhering to the principles of truthful speech, promoting social cohesion and unity, advocating for the rights of the oppressed, and promoting moral and ethical values, media can help to create a more just and equitable society in accordance with Islamic teachings.

27: Technology and Social Justice in Islamic Context

Technology plays a significant role in promoting social justice in Islamic contexts by providing tools and platforms for addressing social issues, empowering marginalized communities, and facilitating access to information and resources. Islamic teachings emphasize the importance of using technology ethically and responsibly to promote justice, fairness, and equality in society.

One of the key ways in which technology promotes social justice in Islamic contexts is by providing access to information and resources. The internet and mobile technologies have revolutionized access to information, allowing people to access news, educational materials, and resources that were previously inaccessible. This has empowered marginalized communities and individuals to access information and resources that can help improve their lives.

Technology also plays a role in promoting social justice by providing platforms for advocacy and activism. Social media platforms, in particular, have become powerful tools for raising awareness about social issues, mobilizing support for causes, and holding authorities accountable. By providing a voice to marginalized communities, technology can help to amplify their concerns and promote positive change.

In addition, technology can help to bridge the gap between urban and rural communities in Islamic contexts. Mobile technologies, for example, can be used to provide healthcare services, educational resources, and agricultural information to rural communities, improving their quality of life and promoting social justice.

Islamic teachings also emphasize the importance of using technology to promote ethical and moral values. The Quran emphasizes the importance of using resources responsibly and avoiding waste, stating, "And do not waste [resources] extravagantly. Indeed, He does not like the wasteful" (Quran 6:141). This principle highlights the importance of using technology in a way that promotes social justice and sustainability.

Overall, technology plays a crucial role in promoting social justice in Islamic contexts by providing access to information and resources, empowering marginalized communities, and facilitating advocacy and activism. By using technology responsibly and ethically, Islamic societies can harness its power to promote justice, fairness, and equality for all members of society.

28: Art and Culture for Social Justice in Islam

Art and culture play a significant role in promoting social justice in Islam by fostering creativity, expression, and dialogue around social issues. Islamic teachings emphasize the importance of art and culture as a means of promoting beauty, harmony, and social cohesion in society.

One of the key ways in which art and culture promote social justice in Islam is by raising awareness about social issues and advocating for positive change. Artists and cultural practitioners often use their work to shed light on social injustices, challenge stereotypes, and promote empathy and understanding among diverse communities. This can help to create a more inclusive and compassionate society where all members are valued and respected.

Islamic art and culture also emphasize the importance of promoting moral and ethical values. Islamic art, such as calligraphy and geometric patterns, often incorporates Quranic verses and themes that promote virtues such as justice, compassion, and humility. This can help to reinforce these values in society and promote a culture of social justice and righteousness.

Furthermore, art and culture can serve as a means of empowerment for marginalized communities in Islamic contexts. By providing a platform for expression and creativity, art can empower individuals to share their stories, perspectives, and experiences, and to challenge the status quo. This can help to amplify the voices of marginalized communities and promote social justice and equality.

In addition, art and culture can promote social cohesion and unity in Islamic societies. Through shared cultural practices, traditions, and artistic expressions, communities can come together to celebrate their diversity and promote understanding and harmony. This can help to bridge divides and promote a sense of belonging and solidarity among diverse communities.

Overall, art and culture play a crucial role in promoting social justice in Islam by raising awareness, promoting moral and ethical values, empowering marginalized communities, and fostering social cohesion. By promoting creativity, expression, and dialogue, art and culture can help to create a more just and equitable society in accordance with Islamic teachings and principles.

29: Leadership and Social Justice in Islamic Teachings

Leadership in Islam is deeply intertwined with the principles of social justice, as outlined in the Quran and the teachings of the Prophet Muhammad (peace be upon him). Islamic teachings emphasize the importance of just and ethical leadership that upholds the rights and dignity of all members of society.

One of the key principles of leadership in Islam is the concept of 'adl', or justice. The Quran emphasizes the importance of justice in leadership, stating, "O you who have believed, be persistently standing firm in justice, witnesses for Allah, even if it be against yourselves or parents and relatives" (Quran 4:135). This verse highlights the importance of leaders being just and fair in their decisions and actions, even if it means going against their own interests or the interests of their loved ones.

Islamic teachings also emphasize the importance of leaders being humble and compassionate. The Prophet Muhammad (peace be upon him) said, "The leader of the people is their servant" (Sunan Abi Dawud). This hadith highlights the importance of leaders serving their communities with humility and compassion, and putting the needs of others before their own.

Another key principle of leadership in Islam is the concept of 'shura', or consultation. The Quran emphasizes the importance of consulting with others in decision-making, stating, "And those who have responded to their lord and established prayer and whose affair is [determined by] consultation among themselves, and from what we have provided them, they spend" (Quran 42:38). This verse highlights the importance of leaders consulting with their communities and seeking their input in decision-making processes.

Overall, leadership in Islam is seen as a responsibility and a trust that must be upheld with integrity, justice, and compassion. Leaders are expected to promote social justice by upholding the rights and dignity of all members of society, consulting with their communities, and serving as role models of ethical and just behavior. By adhering to these principles, leaders in Islamic societies can help to create more just and equitable societies that uphold the values of Islam.

30: Ethics of War and Peace in Islam

The ethics of war and peace in Islam are guided by the principles outlined in the Quran and the teachings of the Prophet Muhammad (peace be upon him). Islamic teachings emphasize the importance of justice, compassion, and mercy in all aspects of life, including times of conflict.

One of the key principles of the ethics of war in Islam is the concept of 'just war', or 'jihad'. Jihad in Islam refers to the struggle to uphold justice and defend the Muslim community from oppression and aggression. The Quran states, "And fight in the cause of Allah those who fight you, but do not transgress. Indeed, Allah does not like transgressors" (Quran 2:190). This verse emphasizes the importance of fighting only in self-defense and with the intention of upholding justice and protecting the innocent.

Islamic teachings also emphasize the importance of respecting the rights of non-combatants and avoiding harm to civilians during times of war. The Prophet Muhammad (peace be upon him) said, "Do not kill women or children or non-combatants and do not kill old people or religious people" (Sunan Abu Dawood). This hadith highlights the importance of protecting the lives and dignity of all individuals, regardless of their status or beliefs.

Furthermore, Islamic teachings emphasize the importance of seeking peace and reconciliation whenever possible. The Quran states, "And if they incline to peace, then incline to it [also] and rely upon Allah. Indeed, it is He who is the Hearing, the Knowing" (Quran 8:61). This verse highlights the importance of seeking peaceful resolutions to conflicts and striving for reconciliation with adversaries.

Overall, the ethics of war and peace in Islam are guided by the principles of justice, compassion, and mercy. Islamic teachings emphasize the importance of fighting only in self-defense and with the intention of upholding justice and protecting the innocent. Additionally, Islamic teachings emphasize the importance of respecting the rights of non-combatants and seeking peace and reconciliation whenever possible. By adhering to these principles, Muslims strive to promote a more just and peaceful world in accordance with the teachings of Islam.

31: Non-violence and Social Justice in Islam

Non-violence, or 'al-silm', is a fundamental principle in Islam that emphasizes peace, harmony, and non-aggression. While Islam permits self-defense and the defense of the oppressed, it strongly emphasizes the use of peaceful means to resolve conflicts and promote social justice. The teachings of Islam encourage followers to seek peaceful solutions and avoid violence whenever possible.

The Quran emphasizes the importance of peaceful behavior and forbearance, stating, "And the servants of the Most Merciful are those who walk upon the earth easily, and when the ignorant address them [harshly], they say [words of] peace" (Quran 25:63). This verse highlights the importance of responding to aggression with peaceful words and actions, rather than with violence or aggression.

The Prophet Muhammad (peace be upon him) also emphasized the importance of non-violence in his teachings and actions. He said, "Do not be people without minds of your own, saying that if others treat you well you will treat them well, and that if they do wrong you will do wrong to them. Instead, accustom yourselves to do good if people do good and not to do wrong (even) if they do evil" (Sunan Ibn Majah). This hadith emphasizes the importance of responding to aggression with kindness and forgiveness, rather than with violence or retaliation.

Islamic teachings also emphasize the importance of promoting peace and reconciliation in society. The Quran states, "And if two factions among the believers should fight, then make settlement between the two. But if one of them oppresses the other, then fight against the one that oppresses until it returns to the ordinance of Allah. And if it returns, then make settlement between them in justice and act justly. Indeed, Allah loves those who act justly" (Quran 49:9). This verse highlights the importance of seeking peaceful resolutions to conflicts and promoting justice and reconciliation among all members of society.

Overall, non-violence is a fundamental principle in Islam that emphasizes peace, harmony, and non-aggression. Islamic teachings emphasize the importance of seeking peaceful solutions to conflicts, promoting justice and reconciliation, and responding to aggression with kindness and forgiveness. By adhering to these principles, Muslims strive to promote social justice and create a more peaceful and harmonious world.

32: Islamic Revivalism and Social Justice

Islamic revivalism, also known as Islamic revival or Islamic awakening, refers to a renewed interest in and adherence to Islamic teachings and principles. This revivalist movement has had a significant impact on social justice in Muslim-majority countries and communities, as it seeks to promote Islamic values and principles as a means of addressing social issues and promoting justice and equality.

One of the key aspects of Islamic revivalism is its emphasis on the importance of Islamic teachings in guiding all aspects of life, including social, political, and economic issues. Islamic revivalists argue that by adhering to Islamic principles, societies can achieve social justice and harmony. This includes upholding the rights of the poor, the oppressed, and the marginalized, and promoting equality and fairness in all aspects of life.

Islamic revivalism also emphasizes the importance of Islamic education and knowledge in promoting social justice. Revivalist movements often advocate for a return to traditional Islamic teachings and scholarship, arguing that a deep understanding of Islamic principles is essential for addressing contemporary social issues. This includes issues such as poverty, inequality, and injustice, which revivalists believe can be addressed through a deeper adherence to Islamic values.

Furthermore, Islamic revivalism often involves a critique of Western influence and values, particularly in the context of colonialism and globalization. Revivalists argue that Western values and practices have contributed to social injustice and inequality in Muslim-majority countries, and advocate for a return to Islamic values as a means of addressing these issues.

Islamic revivalism has had a significant impact on social justice in Muslim-majority countries and communities. Revivalist movements have been instrumental in advocating for the rights of the poor and marginalized, promoting education and literacy, and addressing issues such as corruption and injustice. By emphasizing the importance of Islamic values and principles in guiding all aspects of life, Islamic revivalism has contributed to the promotion of social justice and equality in Muslim-majority countries and communities.

33: Islamic Feminism and Social Justice

Islamic feminism is a movement that seeks to promote gender equality and justice within an Islamic framework. It draws on Islamic teachings and principles to challenge patriarchal interpretations of Islam and advocate for women's rights and empowerment. Islamic feminism is rooted in the belief that Islam, as a religion, is inherently egalitarian and that it promotes the dignity, rights, and agency of all individuals, regardless of gender.

One of the key principles of Islamic feminism is the belief in the equality of men and women in the eyes of God. Islamic feminists argue that while men and women may have different roles and responsibilities, they are equal in terms of their spiritual worth and their rights before God. They advocate for a reinterpretation of Islamic texts and teachings to promote gender equality and to challenge traditional interpretations that discriminate against women.

Islamic feminists also advocate for women's rights in areas such as education, employment, and political participation. They argue that Islam promotes the education of both men and women and that women should have the same opportunities as men to pursue education and knowledge. They also advocate for women's rights in the workplace, arguing that women should have the right to work and to receive equal pay for equal work. Additionally, Islamic feminists advocate for women's participation in politics and decision-making processes, arguing that women should have a voice in shaping the policies and laws that affect their lives.

Islamic feminism also seeks to address issues such as domestic violence, forced marriage, and other forms of gender-based violence. Islamic feminists argue that Islam prohibits violence against women and that it promotes the dignity and well-being of all individuals. They advocate for laws and policies that protect women from violence and that ensure their rights are upheld.

Overall, Islamic feminism is a movement that seeks to promote gender equality and justice within an Islamic framework. It draws on Islamic teachings and principles to challenge patriarchal interpretations of Islam and to advocate for women's rights and empowerment. By advocating for a reinterpretation of Islamic texts and teachings, Islamic feminists seek to create a more just and equitable society for all individuals, regardless of gender.

34: Youth Engagement for Social Justice in Islam

Youth engagement for social justice in Islam is a dynamic and vital aspect of community development and progress. Islamic teachings emphasize the importance of youth as the future of society and encourage them to actively engage in promoting social justice and positive change.

One of the key aspects of youth engagement for social justice in Islam is the concept of 'ijtihad', or independent reasoning. Islam encourages young people to use their intellect and creativity to address social issues and contribute to the betterment of society. This includes promoting justice, fairness, and equality in all aspects of life.

Islamic teachings also emphasize the importance of activism and advocacy for social justice. The Prophet Muhammad (peace be upon him) encouraged young people to stand up for justice and speak out against injustice. He said, "Help your brother, whether he is an oppressor or he is oppressed" People asked, "O Allah's Messenger (peace be upon him)! It is all right to help him if he is oppressed, but how should we help him if he is an oppressor?" The Prophet (peace be upon him) said, "By preventing him from oppressing others." (Sahih Bukhari) This hadith highlights the importance of standing up against oppression and promoting justice, even if it means challenging authority or the status quo.

Furthermore, Islamic teachings emphasize the importance of community service and volunteering as a means of promoting social justice. The Prophet Muhammad (peace be upon him) said, "The best of people are those who are most beneficial to people" (Al-Mu'jam al-Awsat). This hadith highlights the importance of serving others and contributing to the well-being of the community as a way to promote social justice and equality.

Youth engagement for social justice in Islam is also about fostering a sense of responsibility and accountability. Islam teaches that individuals are responsible for their actions and that they will be held accountable for how they treat others. This encourages young people to be mindful of their actions and to strive to promote justice and fairness in all aspects of their lives.

Overall, youth engagement for social justice in Islam is about empowering young people to become active agents of change in their communities. By promoting the values of justice, fairness, and equality, Islam encourages young people to work towards creating a more just and equitable society for all.

35: The Future of Social Justice in Islamic Thought

The future of social justice in Islamic thought is a topic of ongoing discussion and debate among scholars, activists, and policymakers. While Islamic teachings provide a strong foundation for promoting social justice, the application of these teachings in contemporary contexts poses challenges and opportunities for the future.

One key aspect of the future of social justice in Islamic thought is the need to address contemporary social issues and challenges. This includes issues such as poverty, inequality, environmental degradation, and human rights violations. Islamic scholars and activists are exploring ways in which Islamic teachings can be applied to these issues to promote greater justice and equity in society.

Another important aspect of the future of social justice in Islamic thought is the role of youth and new generations in promoting social justice. Young Muslims around the world are increasingly engaging with Islamic teachings and using them as a framework for promoting social change. This includes advocating for gender equality, environmental sustainability, and economic justice, among other issues.

Technology also plays a role in shaping the future of social justice in Islamic thought. The internet and social media have provided new platforms for Muslims to engage with Islamic teachings and to advocate for social justice. This includes using digital platforms to raise awareness about social issues, mobilize support for causes, and hold authorities accountable.

Furthermore, the future of social justice in Islamic thought is also influenced by global trends and developments. As the world becomes more interconnected, Muslims are increasingly engaging with diverse perspectives and ideas about social justice. This includes learning from the experiences of other cultures and societies and adapting Islamic teachings to address new and emerging challenges.

Overall, the future of social justice in Islamic thought is dynamic and evolving. It is shaped by ongoing dialogue, engagement, and activism among Muslims around the world. By drawing on the rich tradition of Islamic teachings and adapting them to contemporary contexts, Muslims can continue to promote social justice and equity in their societies and beyond.

36: Critiques and Reforms in Islamic Thought for Social Justice

Critiques and reforms in Islamic thought for social justice are essential aspects of addressing contemporary challenges and ensuring that Islamic teachings are applied in a way that promotes justice, fairness, and equality in society. These critiques and reforms often stem from a desire to reconcile traditional Islamic teachings with modern realities and to address perceived shortcomings or misinterpretations of Islamic principles.

One of the key critiques in Islamic thought for social justice is the need to address gender inequality. While Islamic teachings emphasize the equality of men and women in the eyes of God, traditional interpretations of Islamic law and practice have often resulted in discriminatory practices against women. Reformers argue for a more egalitarian interpretation of Islamic teachings that promotes gender equality in all aspects of life.

Another critique in Islamic thought for social justice is the need to address economic inequality. Islamic teachings emphasize the importance of social welfare and charity, but critics argue that these principles are not always implemented effectively in Muslim-majority countries. Reformers advocate for policies and practices that promote economic justice, such as fair distribution of wealth and resources, and support for the poor and marginalized.

Critiques and reforms in Islamic thought for social justice also extend to issues such as human rights, environmental sustainability, and governance. Reformers argue for a more holistic and inclusive interpretation of Islamic teachings that takes into account the broader social, economic, and environmental impacts of individual and collective actions.

Reformers also emphasize the importance of ijtihad, or independent reasoning, in interpreting Islamic teachings for social justice. They argue that ijtihad allows for a dynamic and flexible approach to Islamic law and practice, which is essential for addressing the complex challenges of the modern world.

Overall, critiques and reforms in Islamic thought for social justice are essential for ensuring that Islamic teachings are applied in a way that promotes justice, fairness, and equality in society. By engaging in ongoing dialogue and debate, Muslims can continue to reinterpret and adapt Islamic teachings to address contemporary challenges and promote social justice and equity in their societies.

37: Comparative Studies of Social Justice in Different Religious Traditions

Comparative studies of social justice in different religious traditions offer valuable insights into the diverse ways in which religions approach issues of justice, equity, and fairness in society. By comparing and contrasting the teachings and practices of different religious traditions, scholars and practitioners can gain a deeper understanding of the common values and principles that underpin social justice across cultures and religions, as well as the unique perspectives and approaches that each tradition brings to the table.

One key aspect of comparative studies of social justice is the exploration of the ethical and moral foundations of social justice in different religious traditions. For example, while Islam emphasizes the concepts of 'adl' (justice) and 'ihsan' (excellence in conduct), Christianity emphasizes the principles of love, compassion, and forgiveness. By comparing these teachings, scholars can gain insights into the ways in which different religious traditions understand and promote social justice.

Another important aspect of comparative studies of social justice is the examination of the role of religious institutions and leaders in promoting social justice. In many religious traditions, religious institutions and leaders play a central role in advocating for social justice and addressing issues such as poverty, inequality, and discrimination. By comparing the approaches of different religious traditions, scholars can gain a better understanding of the ways in which religious institutions can contribute to social justice in society.

Comparative studies of social justice also provide an opportunity to explore the ways in which religious teachings and practices intersect with political, economic, and social structures. For example, in some religious traditions, there is a strong emphasis on the importance of social welfare and charity, which can influence the development of social policies and programs. By comparing these approaches, scholars can gain insights into the ways in which religious teachings can shape social structures and institutions.

Overall, comparative studies of social justice in different religious traditions offer a valuable opportunity to explore the common values and principles that underpin social justice across cultures and religions, as well as the unique perspectives and approaches that each tradition brings to the table. By engaging in these studies, scholars and practitioners can gain a deeper understanding of the ways in which religious teachings and practices can contribute to a more just and equitable society.

38: Advocacy and Activism for Social Justice in Islam

Advocacy and activism for social justice in Islam involve efforts to promote fairness, equality, and human rights based on Islamic principles and teachings. Islamic advocacy and activism focus on addressing social, economic, political, and environmental issues affecting communities, with a goal of creating a more just and equitable society.

One of the key aspects of advocacy and activism for social justice in Islam is the concept of 'amr bil ma'ruf wa nahy anil munkar', which means enjoining what is right and forbidding what is wrong. This concept is derived from the Quranic verse, "Let there arise out of you a group of people inviting to all that is good (Islam), enjoining Al-Ma'ruf (i.e. Islamic Monotheism and all that Islam orders one to do) and forbidding Al-Munkar (polytheism and disbelief and all that Islam has forbidden)" (Quran 3:104). Islamic advocacy and activism involve encouraging positive actions and discouraging negative ones in society.

Islamic advocacy and activism also emphasize the importance of standing up against injustice and oppression. The Prophet Muhammad (peace be upon him) said, "Help your brother, whether he is an oppressor or he is oppressed." People asked, "O Allah's Messenger (peace be upon him)! It is all right to help him if he is oppressed, but how should we help him if he is an oppressor?" The Prophet (peace be upon him) said, "By preventing him from oppressing others." (Sahih Bukhari) This hadith highlights the importance of advocating for justice and fairness, even if it means challenging authority or the status quo.

Furthermore, advocacy and activism for social justice in Islam often involve addressing issues such as poverty, inequality, discrimination, and human rights violations. Islamic teachings emphasize the importance of helping the poor and needy, promoting equality and justice, and standing up against oppression and injustice. Muslims are encouraged to engage in acts of charity, volunteerism, and advocacy to address these issues and promote social justice.

Overall, advocacy and activism for social justice in Islam are rooted in the teachings of Islam, which emphasize the importance of promoting justice, fairness, and equality in society. By engaging in advocacy and activism based on Islamic principles, Muslims can work towards creating a more just and equitable society for all.

39: Spiritual Dimensions of Social Justice in Islam

The spiritual dimensions of social justice in Islam are rooted in the belief that social justice is not just a matter of worldly concern, but also a spiritual imperative. Islamic teachings emphasize that acts of social justice are not only beneficial for society, but also essential for one's spiritual growth and development.

One of the key spiritual dimensions of social justice in Islam is the concept of 'sadaqah', or voluntary charity. The Quran emphasizes the importance of giving to those in need, stating, "The example of those who spend their wealth in the way of Allah is like a seed [of grain] which grows seven spikes; in every spike is a hundred grains. And Allah multiplies [His reward] for whom He wills" (Quran 2:261). This verse highlights the spiritual benefits of giving to those in need, as it is seen as a means of purifying one's wealth and earning the pleasure of Allah.

Islamic teachings also emphasize the importance of treating others with kindness and compassion. The Prophet Muhammad (peace be upon him) said, "None of you truly believes until he loves for his brother what he loves for himself" (Sahih Bukhari). This hadith highlights the importance of empathy and compassion in Islam, and emphasizes the spiritual benefits of treating others with fairness and kindness.

Furthermore, the concept of 'tawhid', or the oneness of Allah, plays a central role in the spiritual dimensions of social justice in Islam. Muslims believe that all human beings are equal in the eyes of Allah, regardless of their race, ethnicity, or social status. This belief emphasizes the importance of promoting justice and equality in all aspects of life, as it is seen as a means of worshiping Allah and fulfilling one's duty as a servant of Allah.

Overall, the spiritual dimensions of social justice in Islam emphasize the importance of treating others with kindness, compassion, and fairness. By engaging in acts of charity, empathy, and justice, Muslims can not only contribute to a more just and equitable society, but also enhance their own spiritual well-being and growth.

40: Articulating a Vision for Social Justice in Muslim Societies

Articulating a vision for social justice in Muslim societies involves envisioning a future where Islamic principles of justice, fairness, and equality are fully realized in all aspects of society. This vision encompasses a commitment to addressing social, economic, political, and environmental issues through the lens of Islamic teachings, with a focus on creating a more just and equitable society for all.

One key aspect of articulating a vision for social justice in Muslim societies is the promotion of Islamic values and principles in governance and public policy. This includes advocating for policies that promote economic justice, gender equality, and human rights, while also ensuring that these policies are in line with Islamic teachings.

Another important aspect of articulating a vision for social justice in Muslim societies is the promotion of education and awareness about Islamic teachings related to social justice. This includes educating individuals about the importance of social justice in Islam, as well as empowering them to advocate for social justice in their communities.

Furthermore, articulating a vision for social justice in Muslim societies involves promoting dialogue and collaboration among diverse stakeholders, including religious scholars, activists, policymakers, and community leaders. This includes fostering partnerships that can help advance social justice goals and address the root causes of injustice in society.

Overall, articulating a vision for social justice in Muslim societies is about envisioning a future where Islamic principles of justice, fairness, and equality are fully realized in all aspects of society. By promoting Islamic values and principles, advocating for policy change, and fostering dialogue and collaboration, Muslims can work towards creating a more just and equitable society for all.

41: Building Coalitions for Social Justice in Islam

Building coalitions for social justice in Islam involves forming alliances and partnerships with individuals, organizations, and communities that share a commitment to promoting justice, fairness, and equality based on Islamic principles. These coalitions work together to address social, economic, political, and environmental issues affecting Muslim communities and societies, with a focus on creating positive change and advancing the cause of social justice.

One key aspect of building coalitions for social justice in Islam is the promotion of unity and solidarity among diverse groups. Islamic teachings emphasize the importance of unity among Muslims, regardless of their cultural, ethnic, or sectarian differences. By building coalitions based on shared values and principles, Muslims can work together to address common challenges and achieve common goals.

Another important aspect of building coalitions for social justice in Islam is the promotion of inclusivity and diversity. Islamic teachings emphasize the importance of respecting and valuing the diversity of human beings, and coalitions for social justice in Islam strive to include individuals and communities from diverse backgrounds. By building coalitions that are inclusive and diverse, Muslims can ensure that a wide range of perspectives and experiences are represented in their efforts to promote social justice.

Furthermore, building coalitions for social justice in Islam involves fostering partnerships with non-Muslims and organizations outside of the Muslim community. Islamic teachings emphasize the importance of justice and fairness for all people, regardless of their religion or background. By working with non-Muslims and other organizations, Muslims can build broader coalitions that can have a greater impact in promoting social justice and addressing common challenges.

Overall, building coalitions for social justice in Islam is about working together with others to promote justice, fairness, and equality based on Islamic principles. By promoting unity, inclusivity, and partnerships with others, Muslims can build strong coalitions that can make a positive difference in their communities and societies.

42: Leadership and Social Justice in Islam

Leadership and social justice are deeply intertwined in Islam, as Islamic teachings emphasize the importance of just and ethical leadership in promoting social justice and fairness in society. In Islam, leadership is not just about holding positions of authority, but also about fulfilling the responsibilities and obligations that come with those positions, particularly in terms of promoting justice, equality, and the well-being of all members of society.

One of the key principles of leadership in Islam is the concept of 'adl', or justice. Islamic teachings emphasize the importance of leaders being just and fair in their decisions and actions, and of upholding the rights and dignity of all individuals, regardless of their background or status. The Quran states, "O you who have believed, be persistently standing firm in justice, witnesses for Allah, even if it be against yourselves or parents and relatives" (Quran 4:135). This verse highlights the importance of leaders being just and fair, even if it means going against their own interests or the interests of their loved ones.

Islamic teachings also emphasize the importance of humility and compassion in leadership. The Prophet Muhammad (peace be upon him) said, "The leader of the people is their servant" (Sunan Abi Dawud). This hadith highlights the importance of leaders serving their communities with humility and compassion, and putting the needs of others before their own.

Furthermore, Islamic teachings emphasize the importance of consultation in leadership. The Quran states, "And those who have responded to their lord and established prayer and whose affair is [determined by] consultation among themselves, and from what we have provided them, they spend" (Quran 42:38). This verse highlights the importance of leaders consulting with their communities and seeking their input in decision-making processes.

Overall, leadership and social justice in Islam are deeply interconnected, as Islamic teachings emphasize the importance of just, compassionate, and consultative leadership in promoting social justice and fairness in society. By adhering to these principles, leaders in Islamic societies can help to create more just and equitable societies that uphold the values of Islam.

43: Restorative Justice in Islamic Ethics

Restorative justice in Islamic ethics is rooted in the principles of mercy, forgiveness, and reconciliation. It emphasizes the restoration of relationships and the healing of harm caused by wrongdoing, rather than punishment or retribution. Restorative justice in Islam is guided by the belief that all individuals are capable of redemption and that the ultimate goal of justice is to restore harmony and balance in society.

One of the key principles of restorative justice in Islamic ethics is the concept of 'ta'aruf', or mutual recognition. This concept emphasizes the importance of recognizing the humanity and dignity of all individuals, including those who have committed wrongdoing. Restorative justice in Islam seeks to bring together victims, offenders, and communities in a process of mutual recognition, understanding, and healing.

Islamic teachings also emphasize the importance of forgiveness in the process of restorative justice. The Quran states, "But if someone is pardoned and reconciles, his reward is due from Allah. He does not like the wrongdoers" (Quran 42:40). This verse highlights the importance of forgiveness in Islam and emphasizes that forgiveness is a virtue that is rewarded by Allah.

Furthermore, restorative justice in Islamic ethics emphasizes the importance of accountability and making amends. Offenders are encouraged to take responsibility for their actions and to make restitution to those they have harmed. This may include apologizing, making financial restitution, or performing acts of service to the community.

Overall, restorative justice in Islamic ethics is guided by the principles of mercy, forgiveness, and reconciliation. It seeks to restore harmony and balance in society by bringing together victims, offenders, and communities in a process of mutual recognition, understanding, and healing. By adhering to these principles, Islamic ethics promotes a holistic approach to justice that seeks to address the root causes of wrongdoing and promote healing and reconciliation in society.

44: Social Justice and Sustainable Development in Islam

Social justice and sustainable development in Islam are closely intertwined, as Islamic teachings emphasize the importance of social justice and environmental stewardship in creating a balanced and equitable society. In Islam, sustainable development is not just about economic growth, but also about ensuring the well-being of current and future generations by promoting justice, equity, and environmental sustainability.

One of the key principles of social justice and sustainable development in Islam is the concept of 'mizan', or balance. Islamic teachings emphasize the importance of maintaining a balance in all aspects of life, including the environment, society, and economy. The Quran states, "And the heaven He raised and imposed the balance. That you not transgress within the balance" (Quran 55:7-8). This verse highlights the importance of maintaining a balance in the natural world and avoiding overexploitation or destruction of the environment.

Islamic teachings also emphasize the importance of social justice in sustainable development. The Quran states, "And those who, when they spend, do so not excessively or sparingly but are ever, between that, [justly] moderate" (Quran 25:67). This verse highlights the importance of moderation and equity in economic activities, and emphasizes the importance of ensuring that resources are distributed fairly among all members of society.

Furthermore, Islamic teachings emphasize the importance of environmental stewardship. The Prophet Muhammad (peace be upon him) said, "The world is sweet and green, and verily Allah has made you stewards in it, and He sees how you acquit yourselves" (Sahih Muslim). This hadith highlights the importance of caring for the environment and ensuring that resources are used wisely and sustainably.

Overall, social justice and sustainable development in Islam are based on the principles of balance, equity, and environmental stewardship. By adhering to these principles, Muslims can work towards creating a more just, equitable, and sustainable society that promotes the well-being of all individuals and future generations.

45: Challenges and Opportunities for Social Justice in Muslim Communities

Challenges and opportunities for social justice in Muslim communities are diverse and complex, reflecting the diverse social, economic, political, and cultural contexts in which Muslim communities exist. These challenges and opportunities are shaped by a range of factors, including historical legacies, geopolitical dynamics, and internal dynamics within Muslim communities.

One of the key challenges for social justice in Muslim communities is the persistence of poverty and inequality. Despite the emphasis on social welfare and charity in Islam, many Muslim-majority countries and communities continue to struggle with high levels of poverty, inequality, and social exclusion. This is often exacerbated by factors such as corruption, weak governance, and lack of access to education and healthcare.

Another challenge for social justice in Muslim communities is the impact of conflict and violence. Many Muslim-majority countries and communities have been affected by conflict, war, and political instability, which have had devastating effects on social cohesion, economic development, and the well-being of individuals and communities. This has created challenges in terms of promoting social justice and addressing the needs of vulnerable populations, such as refugees and internally displaced persons.

Furthermore, social justice in Muslim communities is also affected by cultural and social norms that may perpetuate discrimination and marginalization. For example, in some Muslim-majority countries, women and religious minorities may face discrimination and limited access to education, employment, and healthcare. Addressing these issues requires challenging entrenched beliefs and practices and promoting greater inclusivity and equality.

Despite these challenges, there are also many opportunities for promoting social justice in Muslim communities. One of the key opportunities is the growing awareness and engagement of young people in promoting social justice and addressing issues such as poverty, inequality, and environmental degradation. Young Muslims around the world are increasingly using social media and other platforms to raise awareness about social justice issues and to mobilize support for positive change.

Another opportunity for social justice in Muslim communities is the role of civil society and non-governmental organizations (NGOs) in advocating for social justice and promoting human rights. Many Muslim-majority countries and communities have vibrant civil society sectors that are actively engaged in promoting social justice and addressing the needs of marginalized populations.

Overall, addressing the challenges and seizing the opportunities for social justice in Muslim communities requires a holistic approach that addresses the root causes of inequality and discrimination, promotes inclusive and equitable development, and empowers individuals and communities to advocate for their rights and dignity.

46: Towards a Just Economic System in Islam

Towards a just economic system in Islam involves applying Islamic principles and teachings to create an economic system that promotes fairness, equity, and social welfare. Islamic economic principles are based on the Quran and the teachings of the Prophet Muhammad (peace be upon him), and emphasize the importance of social justice, ethical behavior, and the equitable distribution of wealth.

One of the key principles of a just economic system in Islam is the prohibition of riba, or usury. The Quran explicitly prohibits the charging of interest, stating, "Those who consume interest cannot stand [on the Day of Resurrection] except as one stands who is being beaten by Satan into insanity. That is because they say, 'Trade is [just] like interest.' But Allah has permitted trade and has forbidden interest" (Quran 2:275). This prohibition is based on the belief that charging interest leads to exploitation and inequality, and is harmful to society as a whole.

Another key principle of a just economic system in Islam is the concept of zakat, or obligatory charity. Muslims are required to give a portion of their wealth to those in need, and this wealth is distributed to the poor, the needy, and other categories of beneficiaries. The Quran states, "And establish prayer and give zakat, and whatever good you put forward for yourselves - you will find it with Allah. Indeed, Allah of what you do, is Seeing" (Quran 2:110). Zakat is seen as a means of redistributing wealth and ensuring that everyone has access to the basic necessities of life.

Furthermore, a just economic system in Islam emphasizes the importance of ethical behavior and fair trade practices. The Prophet Muhammad (peace be upon him) said, "The seller and the buyer have the right to keep or return goods as long as they have not parted or till they part; and if both the parties spoke the truth and described the defects and qualities [of the goods], then they would be blessed in their transaction, and if they told lies or hid something, then the blessings of their transaction would be lost" (Sahih Muslim). This hadith highlights the importance of honesty, transparency, and fairness in economic transactions.

Overall, a just economic system in Islam is based on principles of fairness, equity, and social welfare. By applying these principles, Muslims can work towards creating an economic system that promotes the well-being of all members of society and ensures that everyone has access to the basic necessities of life.

47: Reconciliation and Social Justice in Islam

Reconciliation and social justice in Islam are intertwined concepts that emphasize the importance of restoring harmony and balance in relationships and society. Islamic teachings emphasize the importance of reconciliation as a means of resolving conflicts, promoting forgiveness, and fostering peace and unity among individuals and communities.

One of the key principles of reconciliation in Islam is the concept of 'sulh', or reconciliation. Islamic teachings emphasize the importance of seeking reconciliation and resolving disputes in a peaceful and just manner. The Quran states, "And if two factions among the believers should fight, then make settlement between the two. But if one of them oppresses the other, then fight against the one that oppresses until it returns to the ordinance of Allah. And if it returns, then make settlement between them in justice and act justly. Indeed, Allah loves those who act justly" (Quran 49:9). This verse highlights the importance of seeking reconciliation and resolving conflicts through peaceful means.

Furthermore, reconciliation in Islam emphasizes the importance of forgiveness and mercy. The Prophet Muhammad (peace be upon him) said, "Shall I not inform you of something more excellent in degree than fasting, prayer and almsgiving (sadaqah)? The people replied: Yes, indeed. He (peace be upon him) said: It is putting things right between people, spoiling them is the shaver (destructive)." (Sunan Abi Dawud) This hadith highlights the importance of reconciling with others and seeking forgiveness as a means of achieving spiritual excellence.

Moreover, reconciliation in Islam also emphasizes the importance of social justice. The Quran states, "O you who have believed, be persistently standing firm in justice, witnesses for Allah, even if it be against yourselves or parents and relatives. Whether one is rich or poor, Allah is more worthy of both. So follow not [personal] inclination, lest you not be just. And if you distort [your testimony] or refuse [to give it], then indeed Allah is ever, with what you do, Acquainted" (Quran 4:135). This verse highlights the importance of standing up for justice and fairness, even if it means going against one's own interests or the interests of loved ones.

Overall, reconciliation and social justice in Islam are interconnected concepts that emphasize the importance of restoring harmony, promoting forgiveness, and upholding justice in relationships and society. By adhering to these principles, Muslims can work towards creating a more peaceful, just, and harmonious society for all.

48: Empowerment and Social Justice in Islam

Empowerment and social justice in Islam are closely linked concepts that emphasize the importance of enabling individuals and communities to achieve their full potential and participate fully in society. Islamic teachings emphasize the importance of empowering individuals through education, economic opportunities, and social support, in order to promote justice, fairness, and equality in society.

One of the key principles of empowerment in Islam is the concept of 'taqwa', or God-consciousness. Islamic teachings emphasize that true empowerment comes from being conscious of Allah and seeking to fulfill one's duties and responsibilities towards Allah and towards others. The Quran states, "O mankind, indeed We have created you from male and female and made you peoples and tribes that you may know one another. Indeed, the most noble of you in the sight of Allah is the most righteous of you. Indeed, Allah is Knowing and Acquainted" (Quran 49:13). This verse highlights the importance of piety and righteousness in Islam, and emphasizes that true empowerment comes from living a life of piety and righteousness.

Furthermore, empowerment in Islam is also closely linked to the concept of 'ijtihad', or independent reasoning. Islamic teachings emphasize the importance of using one's intellect and reasoning to understand and interpret Islamic teachings, and to seek solutions to social, economic, and political challenges. The Quran states, "So ask the people of the message if you do not know" (Quran 16:43). This verse highlights the importance of seeking knowledge and using one's intellect to seek solutions to problems.

Moreover, empowerment in Islam also emphasizes the importance of social justice. The Quran states, "Indeed, Allah orders justice and good conduct and giving to relatives and forbids immorality and bad conduct and oppression. He admonishes you that perhaps you will be reminded" (Quran 16:90). This verse highlights the importance of justice and fairness in Islam, and emphasizes that true empowerment comes from upholding justice and fairness in society.

Overall, empowerment and social justice in Islam are interconnected concepts that emphasize the importance of enabling individuals and communities to achieve their full potential and participate fully in society. By adhering to these principles, Muslims can work towards creating a more just, fair, and equitable society for all.

49: Cultural Diversity and Social Justice in Islam

Cultural diversity and social justice in Islam are interconnected concepts that emphasize the importance of respecting and valuing the diversity of cultures, languages, and traditions within Muslim communities and societies. Islamic teachings emphasize the importance of justice, fairness, and equality for all individuals, regardless of their cultural background or identity.

One of the key principles of cultural diversity and social justice in Islam is the concept of 'ummah', or community. Islamic teachings emphasize that all Muslims are part of a single community, regardless of their cultural or ethnic background. The Quran states, "And hold firmly to the rope of Allah all together and do not become divided. And remember the favor of Allah upon you - when you were enemies and He brought your hearts together and you became, by His favor, brothers. And you were on the edge of a pit of the Fire, and He saved you from it. Thus does Allah make clear to you His verses that you may be guided" (Quran 3:103). This verse highlights the importance of unity and solidarity among Muslims, regardless of their cultural or ethnic differences.

Furthermore, cultural diversity and social justice in Islam are also linked to the concept of 'ijtihad', or independent reasoning. Islamic teachings emphasize the importance of using one's intellect and reasoning to understand and interpret Islamic teachings, and to seek solutions to social, economic, and political challenges. The Quran states, "So ask the people of the message if you do not know" (Quran 16:43). This verse highlights the importance of seeking knowledge and using one's intellect to seek solutions to problems.

Moreover, cultural diversity and social justice in Islam also emphasize the importance of tolerance and mutual respect. The Prophet Muhammad (peace be upon him) said, "The believers in their mutual kindness, compassion, and sympathy are just like one body. When one of the limbs suffers, the whole body responds to it with wakefulness and fever" (Sahih al-Bukhari). This hadith highlights the importance of empathy and compassion in Islam, and emphasizes the importance of treating others with kindness and respect, regardless of their cultural or ethnic background.

Overall, cultural diversity and social justice in Islam are interconnected concepts that emphasize the importance of respecting and valuing the diversity of cultures, languages, and traditions within Muslim communities and societies. By adhering to these principles, Muslims can work towards creating a more inclusive, tolerant, and just society for all.

50: Conclusion: The Imperative of Social Justice in Islamic Faith and Practice

The imperative of social justice in Islamic faith and practice is a fundamental aspect of the teachings of Islam. Throughout the Quran and the teachings of the Prophet Muhammad (peace be upon him), there is a clear emphasis on the importance of justice, fairness, and equality for all individuals and communities. Social justice is not just a moral or ethical imperative in Islam, but also a religious duty and a core principle that underpins the entire Islamic faith.

One of the key teachings of Islam regarding social justice is the concept of 'adl', or justice. The Quran emphasizes the importance of justice in many verses, such as, "Indeed, Allah orders justice and good conduct and giving to relatives and forbids immorality and bad conduct and oppression. He admonishes you that perhaps you will be reminded" (Quran 16:90). This verse highlights the importance of justice in Islam and emphasizes that justice is a central tenet of the faith.

Furthermore, the Prophet Muhammad (peace be upon him) emphasized the importance of justice in his teachings and actions. He said, "Help your brother, whether he is an oppressor or he is oppressed." People asked, "O Allah's Messenger (peace be upon him)! It is all right to help him if he is oppressed, but how should we help him if he is an oppressor?" The Prophet (peace be upon him) said, "By preventing him from oppressing others." (Sahih Bukhari) This hadith highlights the importance of standing up against injustice and oppression, even if it means challenging authority or the status quo.

Moreover, the imperative of social justice in Islamic faith and practice is not just limited to individual actions, but also extends to the social, economic, and political structures of society. Islamic teachings emphasize the importance of creating a just and equitable society where everyone has access to the basic necessities of life, such as food, shelter, education, and healthcare.

In conclusion, the imperative of social justice in Islamic faith and practice is a central and fundamental aspect of the teachings of Islam. It emphasizes the importance of justice, fairness, and equality for all individuals and communities, and serves as a guiding principle for Muslims in their interactions with others and their efforts to create a more just and equitable society. By adhering to these teachings, Muslims can work towards fulfilling their religious duty and creating a world where social justice is a reality for all.

About the author Binish Shah

Binish Shah Expertise in sales management extends globally, where she crafts strategic approaches for various international companies. Her role involves devising tailored strategies for companies traversing the globe, leveraging her extensive sales experience and understanding of diverse markets.

Beyond her professional prowess, Binish Shah passion for personal development shines. She embraces mindfulness, honing its practical applications for enhanced focus and mental well-being. Her journey includes conquering stage fright, mastering public speaking, and fostering personal growth.

Financially astute, Binish Shah adeptly manages personal finances, drawing on her understanding of influence and persuasion across both professional and personal spheres.

Despite a busy schedule, maintaining a healthy lifestyle remains paramount to Binish Shah. She not only creates nutritious meals swiftly but also explores meditation practices for inner tranquility.

Emphasizing healthy relationships through effective communication and boundaries, Binish Shah values continual self-reflection and personal growth.

Networking stands as a cornerstone for her career advancement. She refines time management skills to maximize productivity and attain her objectives.

Her grasp of investment fundamentals enables informed financial decisions. To maintain equilibrium, Binish Shah delves into stress reduction techniques like mindfulness, yoga, and meditation, fostering a balanced mindset.

Yours Sincerely

Binish Shah